SMART WORDS
— READER —

ROCKS AND MINERALS

Judith Bauer Stamper

SCHOLASTIC INC.
New York Toronto London Auckland
Sydney Mexico City New Delhi Hong Kong

What are SMART WORDS?

Smart Words are frequently-used words that are critical to understanding concepts taught in the classroom. The more Smart Words a child knows, the more easily he or she will grasp important curriculum concepts. Smart Words readers introduce these key words in a fun and motivational format while developing important literacy skills. Each new word is highlighted, defined in context, and reviewed. Engaging activities at the end of each chapter allow readers to practice the words they have learned.

ISBN 978-0-545-28544-5

Packaged by Q2AMedia

Copyright © 2010 by Scholastic Inc.

Photo credits: t= top, b= bottom, l= left, r= right

Cover Page: Jim Langford/Istockphoto, Samotrebizan/Shutterstock, Yury Kosourov/Shutterstock, Andrew Silver/U.S. Geological Survey, Bragin Alexey/Shutterstock, Oymtu, Hal_P/Shutterstock, Nicholas Sutcliffe/Shutterstock, Dragan Trifunovic/Shutterstock.
Title Page: David Woods/Shutterstock.
Content Page: Mike Norton/Shutterstock.

4-5: D.L. Peck. Frontispiece/U.S. Geological Survey; 5: Bragin Alexey/Shutterstock; 7: Andrea Danti/Shutterstock; 8t: Caitlin Mirra/Shutterstock; 8b, 8-9: Leene/Shutterstock; 9t: Juliengrondin/Shutterstock; 9b, 16-17: Doug Lemke/Shutterstock; 10: Richard Thornton/Bigstock; 11: Marcy J. Levinson/Shutterstock; 12-13: Javarman/Shutterstock, Madmanmoe/Istockphoto; 13: Joe Gough/Shutterstock; 14-15, 30-31: Jim Lopes/Shutterstock; 16-17: Mike Norton/Shutterstock; 17: Bragin Alexey/Shutterstock, Oymtu, Don Nichols/Istockphoto, Shambhu Prakash; 18bl: Jose Gil/Shutterstock; 18bc: Jim Lopes/Shutterstock; 18br: David Woods/Shutterstock; 19: Shutterstock; 20: Michael J Thompson/Shutterstock; 21: Albo/Shutterstock; 22, 23: Nicholas Sutcliffe/Shutterstock; 23: Dmitriyd/Shutterstock, Hal_P/Shutterstock, Andrew Silver/U.S. Geological Survey, Pz Axe/Shutterstock, Yury Kosourov/Shutterstock, Dragan Trifunovic/Shutterstock, Manamana/Shutterstock, Andrew Silver/U.S. Geological Survey, Terry Davis/Shutterstock; 24: Photolibrary, Manamana/Shutterstock, Antonio S./Shutterstock, J. Helgason/Shutterstock; 25: Keith McIntyre/Shutterstock; 26: Dale Woodall/Bigstockphoto; 27: Bragin Alexey/Shutterstock, Pablo Romero/Shutterstock, Dmitriyd/Shutterstock, Fedorov Oleksiy/Shutterstock, Richard Cano/Istockphoto, Sergey Lavrentev/Shutterstock, Don Nichols/Istockphoto, Olegusk/Shutterstock, Yury Kosourov/Shutterstock; 28: Shutterstock; 29: Jack Novak/Superstock/Photolibrary.

Q2AMedia Art Bank: 15.

12 11 10 9 8 7 6 5 4 3 2 1   10 11 12 13 14 15/0

Printed in the U.S.A.
First printing, September 2010

Table of Contents

Chapter 1

Earth Rocks!

You can kick rocks, collect rocks, and even skip rocks across a pond. But rocks are much more than stones you find on the ground. In fact, rocks make up most of planet Earth!

HUGE chunks of rock make up mountains. Tiny pieces of rock make up sand. Wherever you walk, rock is somewhere beneath your feet. Yes, Earth really rocks!

SMART WORDS

rock a solid mixture of minerals that makes up Earth

mineral a non-living, natural material that is the building block of rocks

Half Dome in Yosemite National Park in California

You already know that rocks are hard and have different shapes and sizes. But did you know they are actually made up of a combination of different things?

The main ingredient in rocks is **minerals**. Minerals are Earth's non-living, natural materials. The types of minerals and how they combine determine what kind of rock will form. A **rock** is a solid mixture of minerals that makes up Earth.

You can start to learn how nature mixes minerals together by looking at this rock. It is a piece of granite. Can you see the three minerals that make up granite?

The pink mineral is feldspar.

The grey mineral is quartz.

The black mineral is mica.

How did the minerals in granite get together? To find out, you must first take a look inside Earth.

We live on the hard, rocky, outer layer of Earth. It's called the **crust**. On average, the crust is 20 miles (32 kilometers) thick. If you compared Earth to an apple, the crust would be the peel.

The next layer down is the **mantle**. The mantle is 1,800 miles (2897 kilometers) thick. It's made up of minerals and rock. Temperatures are so high that the rock melts! The red-hot liquid rock is called **magma**.

At the very center of Earth is the core. It's mainly made of iron. The outer core is liquid, but the inner core is solid. Temperatures here are as hot as the sun's surface!

SMART WORDS

crust   the outer layer of Earth

mantle   the layer of Earth under the crust

magma   melted rock in the Earth's mantle

The layers of Earth work together like a giant rock factory. But how does the factory work? Where does Earth get the materials to make new rocks? The answer may surprise you. The Earth recycles!

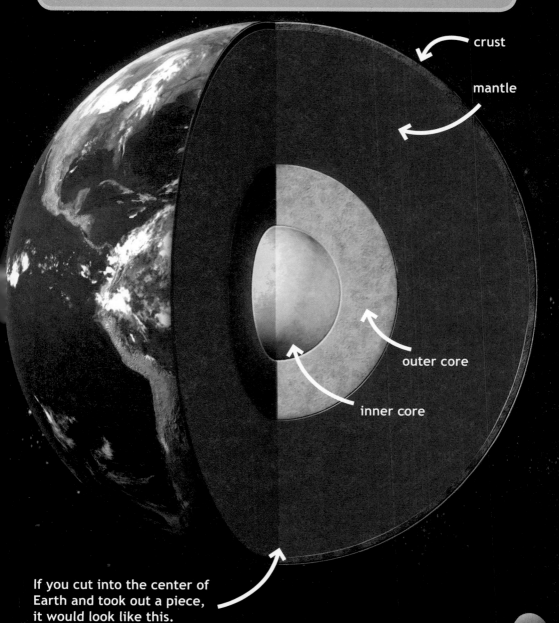

crust

mantle

outer core

inner core

If you cut into the center of Earth and took out a piece, it would look like this.

When you recycle an aluminum can, it gets crushed, melted, and made into a new product. Earth's **rock cycle** works in a similar way. The rock cycle moves materials between the layers of Earth to recycle old rock into new rock! Follow the diagram to see how this works.

The Rock Cycle

Start here and follow the arrows.

Over time, rain, ice, and wind break down huge rocks into tiny pieces called **sediment**. This process is called **weathering**.

Wind and water carry the sediment away and deposit it in a new place. Layers of sediment pile on top of each other, pushing down on the older layers. Water mixes with minerals to cement the particles together, forming rock.

If a rock gets pushed all the way into the mantle, it melts! It is now magma. When it escapes to Earth's surface through a volcano, it bursts out as red-hot lava. As the lava cools, a new rock forms! Weathering begins right away, continuing the rock cycle.

As the bottom layers of sediment get pushed deep into the crust and upper mantle, temperatures and pressure are tremendous. They are tremendous enough to actually change one type of rock into another!

SMART WORDS

rock cycle continuous changing of rock from one type to another

sediment small pieces of sand, mud, pebble, and the remains of dead plants and animals

weathering wearing away of rock over time by water, wind, heat, and ice

Use your SMART WORDS

Match each description with the correct Smart Word.

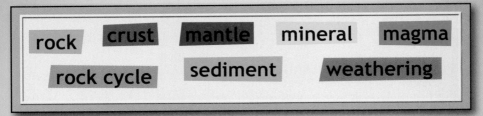

rock   crust   mantle   mineral   magma

rock cycle   sediment   weathering

1. the outer layer of Earth

2. the solid mixture of minerals that makes up Earth

3. the layer of Earth under the crust

4. a non-living, natural material that makes up rocks

5. small pieces of sand, mud, pebbles, and the remains of dead plants and animals

6. the way that water, wind, heat, and ice change rocks over time

7. melted rock in the Earth's mantle

8. the continuous changing of rock from one type to another

Answers on page 32

Talk Like a Scientist

Tell what you know about rocks. Use your Smart Words from the list above and give at least three facts.

SMART FACTS

Did You Know?

The faces of four presidents are carved into the granite rock of Mount Rushmore in South Dakota. They are George Washington, Thomas Jefferson, Theodore Roosevelt, and Abraham Lincoln.

That's Amazing!

Even presidential power can't stop the forces of weathering! More than 40 years after Mt. Rushmore was completed, the presidents' faces began to wear away. Using plaster and metal rods, workers were able to repair the damage.

Mt. Rushmore in the Black Hills of South Dakota

How Big?

Stone Mountain in Georgia has another incredible carving in granite. This carving of Stonewall Jackson, Robert E. Lee, and Jefferson Davis is about the size of 3 football fields, or 3 acres.

Chapter 2

ROCK STARS

All rocks are grouped into three different types — igneous, sedimentary, and metamorphic.

Igneous Rocks: From Liquid Fire

Rocks made from melted rock that has cooled and hardened are called **igneous rocks**. The word *igneous* means "made of fire." Igneous rocks make up 90 percent of the Earth.

What an igneous rock looks like depends on the type of **lava** it is made from and how fast or slow it cools. Lava is melted rock from inside the Earth that reaches the surface.

The faster lava cools, the smoother it will be. Some magma travels up toward Earth's crust but never breaks through the surface. Deep within the crust, it cools very slowly. The slower it cools, the rougher the rock will be.

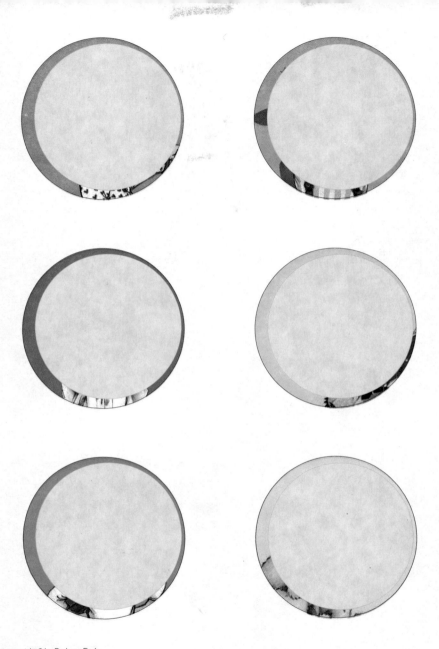

ISBN S-TK5-16924-0 PO# 97031

Crystal Gazing

Minerals that make up rocks are made of crystals. Crystals are solid shapes with flat surfaces lined up in repeating patterns.

You can tell if an igneous rock formed above ground or underground by looking at the size of its crystals! If the minerals in a rock cool quickly, the crystals do not have time to grow big. If the minerals cool slowly, the crystals have time to grow much bigger.

Basalt is a smooth rock with tiny crystals. It cooled quickly on the surface of Earth.

Granite is a rough rock with big crystals. It cooled slowly under the Earth's crust.

SMART WORDS

igneous rock   rock that forms when magma cools and becomes solid

lava   melted rock from inside the Earth that reaches the surface

crystal   a solid shape with flat surfaces that line up in a repeating pattern

Sedimentary Rocks: Layer by Layer

Often, sediment that has broken off rock ends up in streams and rivers that carry it to the ocean. Once there, the sediment drifts to the ocean floor. Over time, layers pile up to form **sedimentary rocks**.

The size and shape of the particles affect how the rock will look. Some sedimentary rocks look like pudding with large pieces of fruit in it. They are sometimes called puddingstones. Sedimentary rocks such as sandstone and shale have very small particles, like grains of sand or dust.

Do you see the layers of color in the sedimentary rock? They are formed by different kinds of sediment and minerals.

Some sedimentary rock, such as limestone, forms from the remains of dead organisms. Instead of rock particles, the hard parts that remain after an organism dies pile up in layers. Look at the diagram to see how limestone forms from the remains of ocean organisms.

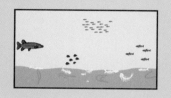 When an ocean creature dies, its soft parts either decay or are eaten. The remaining hard parts sink to the ocean floor.

 Layers of bones and shell pile up on top of each other.

 The weight of the top layers, as well as the weight of the water, presses down on the bottom layers. The pressure squeezes the bottom layers together to form sedimentary rock.

SMART WORDS

sedimentary rock rock formed by layers of sediment in the ground being pressed together

Metamorphic Rocks: Changing Form

Remember that part of the rock cycle where one rock changes into another type of rock? This isn't magic — it's science!

Metamorphic rock is rock that has changed from one form to another. In fact, the name means "changed in form."

Metamorphic rock forms deep beneath Earth's surface, where there is great heat and pressure. High heat and pressure can change the crystal structure of the minerals in a rock. When this happens, it changes into a different kind of rock!

Sometimes heat and pressure makes the minerals separate into layers. In rocks such as gneiss, they can be seen in bands of light and dark colors. These bands may get twisted and bent.

Metamorphic Rocks

Before → After	
Granite → **Gneiss**	Gneiss has bands of light and dark minerals. The bands are twisted by pressure inside the Earth.
Limestone → **Marble**	Marble has millions of pale crystals that have been tightly packed together by heat and pressure within the Earth.

SMART WORDS

metamorphic rock rock that has changed from one kind of rock to another

Use your SMART WORDS

Read each clue. Choose the Smart Word it describes.

igneous rock   sedimentary rock   lava

metamorphic rock   crystal

1. I am rock that forms when hot magma cools and becomes a solid.

2. I am melted rock from inside the Earth that reaches the surface.

3. I am rock that has changed from one kind of rock to another.

4. I am a solid shape with flat surfaces lined up in a repeating pattern.

5. I am rock formed by layers of sediment in the ground being pressed together.

Answers on page 32

Talk Like a Scientist

Look at each of the photographs below. Tell what kind of rock it is and how you know.

SMART FACTS

A hoodoo formation found in Bryce Canyon in Utah.

Did You Know?

What is a hoodoo? It is a tall, skinny spire that rises up from the ground. Hoodoos are made of sandstone that has been shaped by the forces of heat, ice, and rain. Some hoodoos are the size of a human. Others are as tall as a 10-story building.

That's Amazing!

Sandstone has many practical uses. It's often used for walkways or stone walls. It's also used for different arts and crafts as it is easily carved. You may even take a drink from fine glassware made from sandstone!

Did You Know?

Navajo Sandstone is a rock formation that spreads across Arizona, Colorado, and Utah. Soaring at times to 2,200 feet (670 meters), it forms the main attractions at places such as Zion National Park and the Grand Staircase-Escalante National Monument.

Chapter 3

Rock Detectives

Are you ready to explore along with a rock detective?

Scientists called **geologists** study rocks and minerals. They use clues in rocks to identify how they formed and how they change. Bring along the words you have learned as you read what rock detectives have discovered!

Black sand beach in Hawaii.

Why does this beach in Hawaii have black sand?

This sand is made up of tiny pieces of igneous rock that formed after a volcano erupted. Over millions of years, heat, rain, and water weathered the rock. It broke into millions of small pieces of black sediment. The black sand collected at the edge of the ocean.

How did the Grand Canyon form?

The Grand **Canyon** was carved from sedimentary rock. A canyon is a deep, narrow valley with steep sides. It took millions and millions of years to build up all the layers of sediment.

The canyon formed when a river cut its way through the soft rock. The river wore down and carried away the rock particles. The canyon became deeper and deeper!

SMART WORDS

geologist a scientist who studies Earth's layers of soil and rock

canyon a deep, narrow river valley with steep sides

Tools of the Trade

How can rock detectives tell one mineral from another?

One of the best ways to identify a mineral is by its **hardness**. Hardness means how easily a mineral can scratch something else or be scratched itself.

A scientist named Friedrich Mohs developed a scale of hardness for minerals in 1812. It is called Moh's Hardness Scale. Scientists still use the scale today!

Moh's Hardness Scale rates the hardness of minerals from 1 to 10. Talc is the softest mineral at number 1. A diamond is the hardest mineral at number 10. A mineral can scratch any mineral with a lower number than its own.

SMART WORDS

hardness how easily a mineral can scratch something or be scratched itself

Moh's Scale of Hardness

Rating	Mineral		Hardness Examples
1	Talc		
2	Gypsum		fingernail 2.5
3	Calcite		penny 3.5
4	Fluorite		
5	Apatite		common knife blade 5.5
6	Feldspar		
7	Quartz		glass 6 to 7
8	Topaz		
9	Corundum		
10	Diamond		

Mineral Mysteries

A rock detective can't always judge a mineral by its color. Some minerals, like tourmaline, can be black, brown, pink, green, or blue. But they can be identified using a streak test. Streak is the color of powder left when you rub a mineral against a rough surface. Even minerals that come in different colors all leave the same color streak.

How to do a streak test:

1. Use the rough back of a white ceramic tile.

2. Rub the mineral across the tile.

3. Check out the color of the streak.

Mineral Name	Color of Streak
tourmaline	white
black hematite	cherry red
gold	gold

A **geode** is another mineral mystery. It looks like a regular rock. But it has a surprise inside.

How Geodes Form

1. Gas bubbles get trapped inside a rock and form a hole.

2. A solution of water and minerals seeps into the hole.

3. Slowly, the water evaporates and leaves behind mineral crystals.

4. More water seeps in carrying different minerals. Different color crystals form inside the geode.

It may look like a regular rock on the outside, but the inside of a geode is filled with beautiful crystals!

SMART WORDS

streak the color of powder left when a mineral is rubbed against a rough surface

geode a rock with a crystal-lined cavity or hole

Be a Rock Hound!

Want a hobby that rocks? Be a **rock hound**. Rock hounds have their own rock collections.

First, collect your rocks. Look in the mountains, on a beach, or in a stream. Look in a park or in your own backyard. Rocks are everywhere!

Next, display your rocks. Make a box with different sections and labels. Or use an egg carton to hold your rocks.

Then, use the pictures on the next page to identify your rocks. If you can't find them here, look in a field guide or on the Internet. Look at their texture, color, and hardness as clues. Put a label on each rock with its name.

Show off your rock collection. Tell people everything you know about rocks.

A Rock and Mineral Collection

granite

quartz

obsidian

sandstone

shale

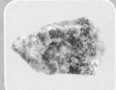
calcite

limestone

basalt

feldspar

SMART WORDS

rock hound a person who collects and identifies rocks and often has a rock collection

Use your SMART WORDS

Answer each question with a Smart Word.

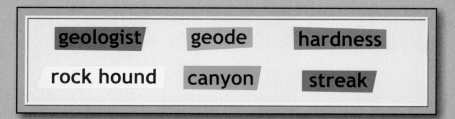

geologist   geode   hardness

rock hound   canyon   streak

1. What scientist studies Earth's layers of soil and rock?

2. What do you call a person who collects rocks?

3. What is a deep, narrow river valley with steep sides?

4. What describes how easily a mineral can scratch something or be scratched itself?

5. What is a rock with a crystal-lined cavity?

6. What is the color of powder left behind when you rub a mineral across a rough surface?

Answers on page 32

Talk Like a Scientist

Diamonds are known for their beauty. How would you describe a diamond to a friend who is interested in rocks and minerals? Use Smart Words in your answer.

Did You Know?

The Smithsonian Institute has one of the largest collections of rocks and minerals. There are 350,000 minerals and 10,000 gems in their National Gem and Mineral Collection.

That's Amazing!

Crater of Diamonds State Park in Arizona is a rock hound haven! For a small fee, visitors can keep any diamond they find! Since 1972, over 21,000 diamonds have been found.

Record Breaker

The Lyndon B. Johnson Space Center in Houston, Texas has an out-of-this-world rock collection. It houses the largest collection of moon rocks brought back from the Apollo space missions.

Among the Smithsonian's collection is the Hope Diamond. It is a 45.54 carat blue diamond!

Glossary

canyon a deep, narrow river valley with steep sides

crust the outer layer of Earth

crystal a solid shape with flat surfaces lined up in a repeating pattern

geode a rock with a crystal-lined cavity

geologist a scientist who studies Earth's layers of soil and rock

hardness how easily a mineral can scratch something or be scratched itself

igneous rock rock that forms when hot molten rock cools and becomes solid

lava melted rock from inside the Earth that reaches the surface

magma melted rock inside the Earth

mantle the layer of Earth under the crust

metamorphic rock a rock that has changed from one kind of rock to another

mineral   a natural material that joins together to form rocks

pressure   the force exerted by pressing on something

rock   a solid mixture of minerals that makes up most of Earth

rock cycle   continuous changing of rock from one type to another

rock hound   a person who collects and identifies rocks and often has a rock collection

sediment   small pieces of sand, mud, pebbles, and the dead remains of plants and animals

sedimentary rock   formed by layers of sediment in the ground being pressed together

streak   the color of powder left when a mineral is rubbed against a rough surface

weathering   the way that water, wind, heat, and ice change rocks over time

Index

SMART WORDS Answer Key

Page 10
1. crust, 2. rock, 3. mantle, 4. mineral, 5. sediment,
6. weathering, 7. magma, 8. rock cycle

Page 18
1. igneous rock, 2. lava, 3. metamorphic rock, 4. crystal,
5. sedimentary rock

Page 28
1. geologist, 2. rock hound, 3. canyon, 4. hardness,
5. geode, 6. streak